FABULOUS ANIMALS

The Story of the Kangaroo

Anita Ganeri

raintree

a Capstone company — publishers for children

Raintree is an imprint of Capstone Global Library Limited, a company incorporated in England and Wales having its registered office at 264 Banbury Road, Oxford OX2 7DY – Registered company number: 6695582

www.raintree.co.uk
myorders@raintree.co.uk

Text © Capstone Global Library Limited 2016
The moral rights of the proprietor have been asserted.

Edited by Linda Staniford
Designed by Philippa Jenkins
Original illustrations © Capstone Global Library Limited 2016
Picture research by Morgan Walters
Production by Victoria Fitzgerald
Originated by Capstone Global Library Ltd
Printed and bound in China

ISBN 978 1 474 71451 8
19 18 17 16 15
10 9 8 7 6 5 4 3 2 1

British Library Cataloguing in Publication Data
A full catalogue record for this book is available from the British Library.

Acknowledgements
We would like to thank the following for permission to reproduce photographs: Alamy: David Reed, 24; Bridgeman Images: National Library of Australia, Canberra, Australia, 7, Natural History Museum, London, UK, 6; Corbis: Charles & Josette Lenars, 12, Hulton-Deutsch Collection, 22; Dreamstime: Jan Pokorný, Cover, Sandbread, 18; Getty Images: Auscape/UIG, 13, Hulton Archive, 5, Mitsuaki/Iwago, 20, Photolibrary, 4, Yva Momatiuk & John Eastcott, 15; Glow Images: Deposit Photos, 23, Steve Bowman, 10; iStockphoto: Houshmand Rabbani, 14; Newscom: STR/REUTERS, 27, TUNS/picture alliance/Arco Images G, 19; Science Source: Wayne G. Lawler, 26; Shutterstock: Dioscoro L. Dioticio, 16, Gianna Stadelmyer, 17, nattanan726, 9, shelley kirby, 21, Totajla, 25; The Trustees of the British Museum, 11; Wikimedia: ArtDaily.com, 8.

We would like to thank Michael Bright for his invaluable help in the preparation of this book.

Every effort has been made to contact copyright holders of material reproduced in this book. Any omissions will be rectified in subsequent printings if notice is given to the publisher.

All the internet addresses (URLs) given in this book were valid at the time of going to press. However, due to the dynamic nature of the internet, some addresses may have changed, or sites may have changed or ceased to exist since publication. While the author and publisher regret any inconvenience this may cause readers, no responsibility for any such changes can be accepted by either the author or the publisher.

Contents

Some words are shown in bold, like this. You can find out what they mean by looking in the glossary.

Kangaroo search

From the 1600s, sailors from Europe began to explore Australia. They saw strange animals that hopped on very long back legs. The sailors did not know what they were.

Sailors saw animals like this one.

This is Captain Cook's ship, *Endeavour*.

In 1770, British explorer Captain James Cook was sailing along the coast of Australia. His ship hit a **coral reef** and had to stop for repairs. One of the ship's scientists, Joseph Banks, went ashore to look for new animals and plants.

Banks saw an animal the size of a greyhound dog, with a long tail. Instead of running on all fours, it hopped very fast on its back legs. The local people called it a "gangurru". Banks called it a "kangaroo".

This is an early drawing of a kangaroo.

6

A few weeks later, the men shot a kangaroo and ate it for dinner. Cook reported that it tasted delicious! Banks took the kangaroo skin and skull back to London to study.

A new animal?

In London, the kangaroo skin was stuffed and put on display. Crowds of people came to see it. Most scientists thought that it must be a **rodent**. They thought it was a giant, hopping rat.

This is a painting of the stuffed kangaroo.

Koalas are marsupials, like kangaroos.

But scientists had never seen a rat with a **pouch** on its body. This was where its babies fed and grew! They decided that it belonged to a group of animals called **marsupials**.

Local knowledge

Of course, the local **indigenous** Australians knew about kangaroos long before the European sailors came. They hunted kangaroos for their meat, using spears, nets and **boomerangs**.

An indigenous Australian hunts with a spear.

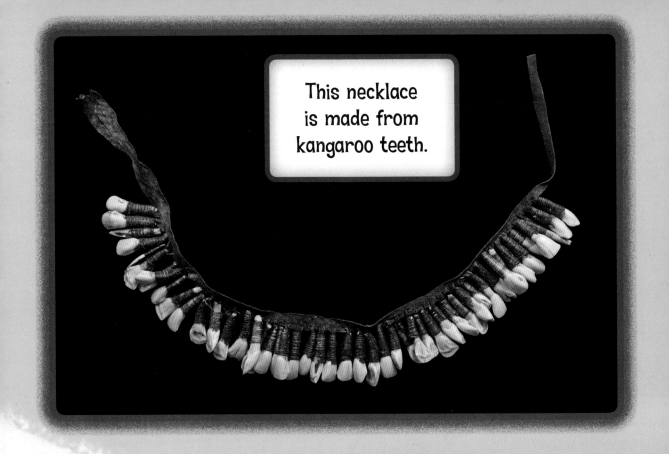

This necklace is made from kangaroo teeth.

The indigenous Australians did not waste any of the kangaroo. They dried the skin and used it to make clothes and bags for carrying water. They used the bones and teeth to make tools and jewellery.

The **indigenous** Australians also have many stories about kangaroos. Most of these stories tell how kangaroos got their unusual features.

The indigenous Australians have many stories about animals.

This is an indigenous Australian rock painting of a kangaroo.

Here is one of their stories:

"Kangaroos once had legs all the same length, and walked on all fours. Then, one day, a kangaroo was resting under a shady tree. A hunter camped nearby. The kangaroo stood up on its back legs and tiptoed away. This is how its legs grew so long and strong."

Meet the kangaroo

The kangaroo that Joseph Banks saw was an eastern grey kangaroo. It lives in woodlands and grasslands. It hides in the bush during the day and comes out to feed at night.

These eastern grey kangaroos are feeding.

male red kangaroo

female red kangaroo

Male red kangaroos are bigger than females.

Red kangaroos live in the desert. They are the biggest **marsupials**. Males can stand more than 2 metres (6.5 feet) tall. That is taller than an adult human. They have short, red-brown fur.

Kangaroo lifestyle

Kangaroos live in small groups, called mobs. As they eat, they listen out for **dingos** and other **predators**. If there is danger, they thump the ground with their feet to warn the others.

This is a mob of kangaroos.

Kangaroos **graze** at night, when it is cooler.

Red kangaroos eat desert plants. Their food is tough and wears their teeth down. When this happens, more teeth move forward. Then, new teeth replace them from behind.

Kangaroos move by hopping on their huge back legs and feet. They use their tails for balance as they leap. At top speed, a kangaroo can hop at over 60 kilometres (37 miles) per hour. Hopping uses up less energy than running on all fours.

A kangaroo can cover 8 metres (26 feet) in one leap.

These kangaroos are "boxing".

Kangaroos sometimes have to defend themselves from attack by other kangaroos. They use their front paws and look as if they are boxing. They also try to kick each other.

A new-born kangaroo, or **joey**, is only about the size of a bumblebee. It crawls up its mother's fur and into her **pouch**. Here, it drinks its mother's milk, and grows bigger and stronger.

This is a new-born joey in its mother's pouch.

This joey is safely back inside its mother's pouch.

When a joey is about six months old, it comes out of the pouch for the first time. It starts to spend more and more time outside. But it quickly dives back in if it feels frightened.

In captivity

Soon after the Europeans arrived in Australia, they began sending live kangaroos back home. It was a long journey by ship, and many of the kangaroos died. In 1791, a kangaroo was sent to London as a gift for the king.

The first kangaroos caused quite a stir!

These kangaroos live in a wildlife park.

Today, there are thousands of kangaroos in zoos and wildlife parks all around the world. They do very well in **captivity**. Many of these kangaroos have been born in captivity.

Kangaroos today

Kangaroos are an important part of Australian life. They have appeared on stamps and coins, in books and on TV. Many Australian companies have kangaroos as their **logos**. Some sports teams are named after kangaroos.

The Australian coat of arms has a kangaroo on it.

This sign warns drivers to watch out for kangaroos on the roads.

Today, there are millions of kangaroos in Australia. Many are killed on the roads every year. Some cars are fitted with "kangaroo whistles". The sounds help to stop kangaroos from crossing the road.

Scientists are still finding out more about kangaroos. At Riversleigh in Australia, they discovered the fossils of **extinct** kangaroos. One had curved, fang-like teeth. The scientists nicknamed it the "fangaroo".

The fossils at Riversleigh are millions of years old.

This is a model of a giant kangaroo that became extinct around 30,000 years ago.

A fossil of a giant kangaroo has been found. It was three times the size of a modern kangaroo. In 2014, scientists discovered that it was too big to hop. It walked on its back legs instead.

Kangaroo timeline

1770

Captain Cook and his crew sail to Australia and see kangaroos.

1771

Banks brings a kangaroo skin to London. It is stuffed and put on display.

1789

British officer, Watkin Tench, writes a detailed description of a kangaroo.

1791

A live kangaroo arrives in London as a gift for the king.

1828

A British scientist, John Morgan, tames a kangaroo. It follows him around like a dog.

1908

The kangaroo features on the Australian coat of arms.

1966

Scientists decide that the kangaroos Banks saw were eastern grey kangaroos.

2000

At the Sydney Olympic Games, the Australian team's logo is a boxing kangaroo.

2014

Scientists discover that the extinct giant short-faced kangaroo probably could not hop but walked instead.

29

Glossary

boomerang curved stick that spins and turns in flight; some boomerangs are made to return to the thrower

captivity condition of being kept in a cage, often in zoos or wildlife parks

coral reef type of land made up of the hardened bodies of corals; corals are small, colourful sea creatures

dingo wild dog that lives in Australia

extinct no longer living; an extinct animal is one that has died out, with no more of its kind

graze feed on grass and plants

indigenous native to a place

joey young kangaroo

logo symbol of an organization's brand

marsupial group of mammals in which the females feed and carry their young in pouches

pouch flap of skin that looks like a pocket in which some animals carry their young

predator animal that hunts other animals for food

rodent mammal with long front teeth used for gnawing; rats, mice and squirrels are rodents

Find out more

Books

Big Red Kangaroo, Claire Saxby (Walker Books Australia, 2015)

Fantastic Facts about Kangaroos, Miles Merchant (CreateSpace, 2015)

The Life Cycle of a Kangaroo, Amy Austen (PowerKids Press, 2015)

Websites

animals.nationalgeographic.com/animals/mammals/red-kangaroo
Facts and figures about kangaroos from the National Geographic website.

animals.sandiegozoo.org/animals/kangaroo-wallaby
Meet the kangaroos at San Diego Zoo.

www.bbc.co.uk/nature/life/Macropod
Information, photos and videos about kangaroos and wallabies.

Index

Australia 4, 5, 22, 24, 25
  Riversleigh 26

Banks, Joseph 5, 6, 7, 14
boxing 19

Cook, Captain James 5, 7

food 17

hopping 4, 6, 18, 27

indigenous Australians 6, 10,
  12, 13

joey (baby kangaroo) 20, 21

kangaroos
  eastern grey 14, 25
  fossil 26, 27
  in captivity 22, 23
  red 15, 17, 25
  whistles 25

marsupials 9, 15
mobs 16

pouch 9, 20, 21
predators 16

size 15
skin 7, 8, 11
speed 18
stories 12, 13

teeth 11, 17

wild kangaroos 14, 15, 25